The Regeneration Machine

Janice Pimm ✹ Dynamo

OXFORD
UNIVERSITY PRESS

TEAM X

Max, Cat, Ant and Tiger are four ordinary children with four extraordinary watches. When activated, their watches allow them to shrink to micro-size.

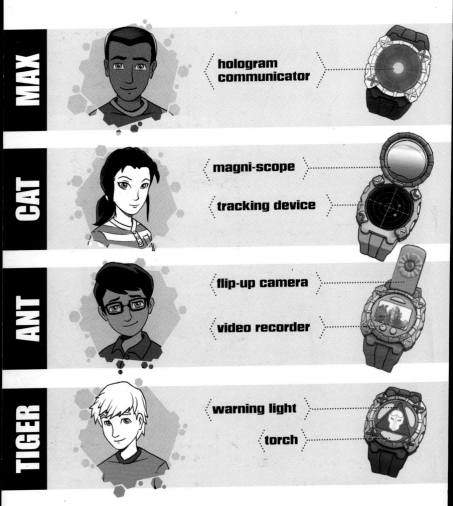

MAX — hologram communicator

CAT — magni-scope, tracking device

ANT — flip-up camera, video recorder

TIGER — warning light, torch

Previously ...

The watches were running low on power. Ant tried to recharge them using a machine that he had invented. However, during this process, something in the watches changed irrevocably.

When all the watches are synchronized, the micro-friends can travel through a rip in the fabric of space and time to other dimensions. Max, Cat, Ant and Tiger have become *rip-jumpers*.

Now there is a problem. The rip has become permanently stuck open ... in Tiger's wardrobe! This leaves Earth – our Earth – open to attack.

Chapter 1 – **The rip is broken!**

A figure emerged through the shimmering portal.

The friends stared in amazement as the glare from the rip faded. Before them stood a tall, beautiful woman. She wore a simple, white suit and her dark, shining hair was tied back with silver thread.

She regarded the friends' astonished faces and smiled. 'Don't be alarmed,' she said soothingly. 'I'm here to help.'

'Help?' stammered Max. 'Help with what?'

The woman stared at him with her piercing, blue eyes. 'Saving your dimension,' she stated calmly. 'If you don't do exactly as I say, then your entire world is doomed.'

The children gasped in horror, then they all began to speak at once.

'What do you mean, *doomed?*' asked Max.

'Do you mean the Krush will come back?' said Tiger. Only moments before the woman arrived, the friends had seen an entire army of the robot warriors disappear back through the dimension rip in Tiger's wardrobe.

'Who *are* you?' demanded Ant.

'And what do you want us to do?' asked Cat.

'Hush!' The woman held up a hand to silence them. 'I will explain everything in good time. First, I must assess the nature of the damage.'

She turned to the rip, which fizzed and crackled, and ran her long, white fingers over its blue edges. 'It is as I feared,' she murmured. 'I am almost too late.'

Mesmerized, the children watched in silence as the woman began to mend the rip. Lines of light like fine spider's silk shot from her fingertips; it looked as if she was stitching the rip back together. When she turned again to face the children, her beautiful face was tense and drawn.

'Oh children, you have no idea of the damage you've caused,' the woman said sternly.

Cat felt the cold weight of dread settle in her stomach.

'Your interference has triggered dire events,' the woman continued.

Max gulped. 'Please tell us what we've done wrong.'

The woman looked grave. 'You have caused a temporal anomaly … an enormous rip in the space-time continuum,' she told them solemnly. 'Every time you passed through the rip on your *adventures*, you made it bigger. Didn't you notice? Didn't you think there might be consequences?'

Ant hung his head. 'We didn't stop to think,' he said in a low voice.

'We'll do whatever you say to put things right,' Tiger added earnestly.

Max looked up and met the woman's piercing gaze. 'We had no idea we were causing any problems,' he said. 'You have my word that we are all truly sorry.'

'Sorry isn't good enough!' replied the woman harshly. She glanced at the rip. 'My repair will not hold for long. The rip is permanently damaged. I'm afraid your world is in terrible danger.'

'You mean the Krush could come back?' asked Ant.

The woman nodded her head slowly. 'Yes, the Krush … and worse than that. *Much* worse.'

'But you said before that you had come to help,' Cat pointed out. 'You said our world would be doomed *unless* we did what you said, so there must be something we can do. Please?'

At this, the woman's face softened a little. 'There is *one* thing …' she said slowly, 'but first, you must understand my story.'

The woman crossed the room. A soft glow emanated from her white suit as she walked. She sat down on the bed and indicated for the children to sit, too. They slumped down on the carpet in front of her.

'My name is Perlest,' she began, her voice becoming light and melodious. 'My story – our story – began long ago. I have a twin sister named Vilana. As children we were inseparable: playing in the sun, running in flower-filled meadows, always laughing. Alas, as we grew older, Vilana *changed*. She developed a terrible craving for power. She became deceitful and malicious. I'm afraid my sister wants power over all dimensions.'

'And the Krush?' asked Tiger.

'The Krush are Vilana's warriors,' said Perlest. 'Vilana can control them, wherever they are. You can't imagine the dreadful things Vilana makes the Krush do in her ruthless quest for power.'

At this point, there was a sudden grating noise from behind the rip. The friends flinched as the top corner of the rip sparked and fizzed. As the rip began to surge, Perlest's fine threads were stretched to breaking point. She sprang from the bed and rushed over to restitch the gap.

'Is that the Krush?' asked Ant in alarm, leaning away from the wardrobe.

'Perhaps. I don't know,' replied Perlest. 'In any case, your world is being watched. We are all in danger.'

'Can the rip be mended ... for good, I mean?' asked Cat.

'There is just one person who could mend the rip,' said Perlest. 'He was once a friend of mine. His name is the Weaver.'

'Then what are we waiting for?' cried Tiger, pulling out his mobile phone from his pocket. 'Can you call him?'

Perlest smiled at Tiger. 'I'm afraid I don't know where he is,' she said. 'The Weaver has not been seen for many years. Some say he is in hiding.' She looked at the children one by one. 'You must find him.'

'We'll do it!' cried Cat, without hesitation.

'Er ... won't you be coming with us?' asked Ant.

Perlest shook her head. 'No, I must stay here and

guard the rip; it is the only way to protect
your dimension.'

'But where should we start looking for him?' Max
was frowning.

'You may be able to pick up his trail in Dimension
7023,' said Perlest. 'There is a rumour of a dimension
traveller visiting there.'

'There's just one problem with this plan,' said
Tiger. 'We never know where we're going to end up
when we rip-jump. Our watches don't take us to a
specific dimension.'

Perlest raised an eyebrow. 'I didn't realize …'

'Well,' said Ant, scratching his head, 'now that
we have a dimension number, I *might* be able to
programme them to get us there. I'll give it a go.'

Perlest clapped her hands together. 'Then it is
settled,' she said brightly. 'You will go to Dimension
7023 and bring back the Weaver!'

Cat unbuckled her watch-strap. Her arm always felt
bare without her watch, but she handed it to Ant. Max
and Tiger did the same.

Ant carefully adjusted each watch in turn until they
were all reading the same four digits: **7023**. Then he
gave the watches back.

Immediately, blue power shone out of the friends'

watches, melting the stitches in the rip that Perlest
had created only minutes before.

'I'll seal the rip behind you,' Perlest told them. 'But
hurry, we don't have much time.'

Together, the friends stepped towards Tiger's
wardrobe and were pulled into the light …

Chapter 2 – The Museum of Children

'Are you sure we're in a different dimension?' Max asked Ant.

The children were standing on the corner of a city street that looked very much like their own world. All along the street, modern shops with bright signs and tall glass windows were interspersed with older, elegant buildings.

Ant checked his watch. 'We're certainly in **7023**,' he said. 'Although I agree it looks just like home!'

'It doesn't *feel* like home though,' said Cat. She was right. The street was much cleaner and tidier than the streets in their own town. It was also eerily quiet. The few adults they could see walked calmly and purposefully with their heads down, barely talking to one another.

The transport was different, too. Every so often, a sleek gold bus glided by with a soft purr. The buses had no wheels. Instead, they floated along just above the ground, carried by pointed gold wings that stuck out of the sides below the windows.

'Definitely not home!' said Tiger, wide-eyed.

'So where do we start looking for the Weaver?' asked Cat.

'We'll have a better chance of finding him if we split u–'. Max was interrupted by the sound of children laughing and shouting. The noise drifted through the air from a few streets away.

'That sounds better!' said Tiger, cocking his head. 'There must be a playground nearby – I vote we go there first. Maybe the local kids will be able to help.'

'Why don't you and Cat go to the playground?' suggested Max. 'Ant and I will try to talk to people on this street. Let's meet back here in an hour.'

The friends headed off in different directions. Sure enough, Cat and Tiger soon came across a playground in a large square. It had rope swings, a giant slide, a zip wire, a huge roundabout and numerous climbing frames. Everywhere, children of all ages were laughing and playing excitedly. On the far side of the park, a few adults wandered amongst the children.

A little girl was swinging along the monkey bars on a climbing frame.

Cat jumped on to the steps of the climbing frame and called out brightly, 'Hello! I'm Cat. What's your name?'

The girl seemed not to hear her. Instead, she jumped off the far end of the monkey bars, ran back to the steps and climbed past Cat, apparently oblivious to her presence.

Cat tried a second time. 'We're looking for someone called the Weaver ...' she began but, once again, the little girl ignored her.

Puzzled, Cat turned to Tiger. He was watching a boy of his own age dribbling a football round the park.

'Do you want to play?' the boy called cheerfully, as he dribbled the ball near to Tiger.

'Sure.' Tiger ran to join the boy but, as he got close,

the boy turned away in the opposite direction. He dribbled his ball in a wide arc and veered back to Tiger.

'Do you want to play?' the boy called again.

'I said yes!' said Tiger, laughing. Running towards the boy, he attempted a tackle.

Tiger's foot passed straight through the football.

'Whoa! Did you see that?' Tiger called to Cat.

Cat had seen. She put out her hand to touch the little girl on the climbing frame. Where she had expected to feel a soft, woolly coat she felt nothing but the pinpricks of static electricity. Her hand passed right through the little girl. Cat shivered. 'They're not children!' she cried. 'They're holograms!'

'Why make holograms of children?' Tiger asked.

There was a crunch of footsteps on the path behind them. Cat and Tiger turned to see an elderly couple leaning on walking sticks. The woman was pointing right at them.

'Oh!' cried the lady. 'Those two look so real!'

'We *are* real,' said Cat.

'Of course you are, dear ...' the lady replied, smiling indulgently.

'It's amazing what they can do with holo-technology these days,' said the old man.

The woman nodded. 'Come on, let's go and get a cup of tea.'

'This is so weird,' said Tiger slowly, watching the couple walk away. 'Let's follow them and see if we can find out what's going on.'

Cat and Tiger followed the couple to a large, square building behind the park. The building had wide stone steps leading up to double glass doors. Above the doors, in gold letters, there was a sign: *Museum of Children.*

'Hey, perhaps this is a museum about childhood through the ages. We might learn something useful about this dimension or even about the Weaver,' suggested Tiger. 'Let's take a look.'

'OK,' Cat agreed, 'but don't do anything to attract attention. This dimension is giving me the creeps!'

Cat and Tiger entered a large hall. They didn't notice the camera just above the door that swivelled towards them as they passed.

Adults were milling around in the hall, reading information on the walls and peering into glass cases containing prams, high chairs and all sorts of children's toys. Holographic children stood around the hall guiding adults to the different displays.

'Tiger!' exclaimed Cat. 'Look at the heading on that poster. It says: *Children: Fact or Myth?'* She took a deep breath. 'Are you thinking what I'm thinking? Is it possible that we're in a dimension with no children?'

At that moment, the museum's doors burst open. A group of men and women in white lab coats – clearly scientists – rushed into the hall and looked around frantically.

Seconds later, the scientists were joined by a man and a woman who looked like police officers: on the back of their jackets were the words **Force 7**.

'Over there!' cried one of the scientists. She was pointing straight at Cat and Tiger.

Chapter 3 – The Goldflight bus

Max and Ant were walking along the high street, searching for news of the Weaver. They hadn't had any luck so far. Max had tried to speak to an elderly lady, but she had just gawped at him in amazement. Then Ant had approached a shopkeeper who had simply stared at the boys, his mouth opening and shutting, seemingly in disbelief.

'I'm not sure we're getting very far,' said Max. 'Let's go back to meet the others.'

As they walked along, several of the buses marked *Goldflight* went past. Ant looked into each bus and soon realized something rather strange.

'Have you noticed that all the buses travelling in that direction are full of old people?' asked Ant, frowning.

'You've given me an idea,' Max replied.

When the next bus stopped, Max jumped up the steps. 'Excuse me,' he called to the driver. 'I'm looking for the Weaver. Do you know anyone with that name?'

The driver looked at Max with wide, astonished

eyes. He stared for a very long time, his brow furrowed as though he was trying to work something out. Then he slowly shook his head.

Max was aware that all eyes on the bus were fixed on him. 'Does anyone know the Weaver?' There was no response, just thirty pairs of old eyes gazing at him in bewilderment.

This is creepy, Max thought as he jumped off the bus. Unknown to Max, the driver picked up his phone and made an urgent call.

Just then, a loud, purring noise echoed all around. A glossy silver-blue car was flying down the street, moving much faster than the buses. With its broad wings, it looked as sleek as a bird of prey.

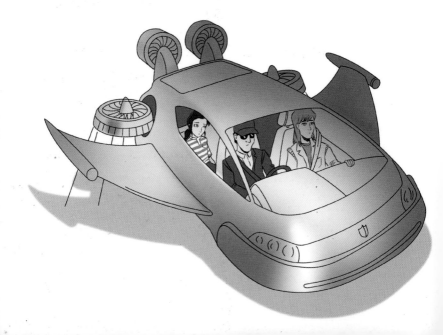

As the car passed by, Ant craned his neck to see inside. The driver wore a stiff-peaked navy cap and beside him sat a woman in a white coat. In the backseat – could it be? – yes! Cat and Tiger sat very still, pale-faced and scared.

Max had seen his friends go by, too. 'We'd better get after them!' he cried.

At that moment, a Goldflight bus glided to a stop next to the boys. Without hesitating, Max and Ant leapt on board.

'We haven't any money,' Max realized with a groan, but the bus driver merely waved them to a seat.

'Hey, this is strange,' observed Ant, strapping a seat belt round his waist. 'All of the other buses were packed, but this one is completely empty.'

At the front of the bus the driver discreetly changed his sign to read: *Not in Service.* He knew this was the most important job of his life, and he didn't want to make any mistakes. The driver pushed his foot down hard on the accelerator. With a jolt, the bus lurched forwards and soared up into the air until it was level with the tops of the buildings. The boys could see right into the busy offices as they flew past.

The bus swayed from side to side as it sped on, flying faster and faster all the time. Despite their seat belts, Max and Ant were thrown about.

Ant could see people at bus stops looking up in astonishment when the driver refused to stop. 'This isn't right …'

Suddenly, the bus veered sharply to the left, sending Max tumbling into Ant.

Max pushed the bell, but the driver didn't slow down. 'Hey,' he called. 'We want to get off!'

The bus zoomed on. The boys were trapped!

At last, the bus drew up in front of a huge, domed building. A sign in front of the building read *Institute of Regeneration*. The driver stopped at a security barrier and got out to talk to the guard.

'Now's our chance!' Max cried. 'Shrink!'

Moments later, the driver and the guard climbed back up the steps to the bus.

'They're in here,' said the driver. 'Look!' He peered into his bus … and got the shock of his life. It was empty.

Micro-sized Max and Ant sneaked through the driver's legs and climbed down the steps.

They looked across at the Insititute.

'We need to get into that building to find out what's going on here,' Max said decisively. 'It looks pretty well guarded though.'

'Look!' cried Ant. Cat and Tiger were being escorted by bulky guards into the Institute.

Max spotted the guard's bag, left slumped on the floor by the bus. 'In there!'

Max and Ant climbed into the bag and waited for another bumpy ride.

Chapter 4 – The observation room

Cat woke gently from what felt like a lovely, long sleep. For a while, she snuggled into deep, soft pillows. Her head felt pleasantly woozy. Gradually, she sat up and opened her eyes. She was in a bedroom. Pretty yellow curtains fluttered in a breeze at the window and bright-white tiles covered the floor. A cuddly rabbit sat in a white chair beside her bed, and the wall above the bed was lined with shelves containing books and games.

Tiger lay dozing on a bed opposite. He opened his eyes and stretched. 'I feel as though I've been sleeping for ages,' he murmured.

'Me too,' said Cat dreamily, 'but how did we get here? This isn't my room … or yours.'

At the mention of his room, Tiger frowned. 'We *were* in my room,' he said thoughtfully. 'I remember a lady called Perlest …'

Suddenly, their memories came flooding back in an almost overwhelming rush: *the rip … Perlest … the Weaver… and the Force 7 police.*

Cat gasped. 'Force 7 must have sent us to sleep somehow.'

Tiger looked at his wrist in horror. 'Our watches! They're gone!'

Cat grabbed her wrist. It had felt bad enough taking off her watch to give to Ant earlier, before rip-jumping. Seeing her bare wrist now made her shiver.

Frantically, Cat and Tiger searched the room, but their watches were nowhere to be found. Without their watches, they would be unable to shrink or return home through the rip.

'We'd better get out of here,' said Cat anxiously.

Tiger staggered across the bedroom towards the door – then *crack!* He fell back suddenly, clutching his head. 'Ow!'

'What is it?' asked Cat in alarm.

Cautiously, Tiger stretched out his hand and his fingers met a hard, cool surface. 'There's a wall of glass.'

In panic, Cat and Tiger felt all the way round the room. Sure enough, they were in a glass box. The pretty windows, bedroom walls and door were all fake.

Cat banged on the wall of glass furiously. 'Let us out!' she demanded, her eyes wide with fear. 'What do you want with us?'

With a *whoosh*, a section of the glass panel suddenly slid back. Through the gap, the children could see a bright-white corridor.

A lady bustled into the room carrying a tea tray. She set it down on a little table decorated with pink flowers.

'Why are you holding us prisoner?' Cat demanded.

'And why did you send us to sleep?' added Tiger.

'Oh, you haven't been asleep for long,' the woman replied. 'It was just to help you settle in.' She picked up a tiny musical box from a dressing table and turned it on. 'We just used this.'

Sweet music filled the room and at once the children felt pleasantly drowsy. Cat shook herself. 'Turn that thing off *now!*' she shouted.

'Now, dear, don't upset yourself,' said the woman. 'I've brought you some nice hot milk and ginger cake.'

'I don't want hot milk,' snapped Cat. 'I want answers. For a start, where are we?'

'You're in the observation room,' the woman replied. 'The scientists can see in, although you can't see out.'

'You're *watching* us?' Tiger asked, indignantly. 'I demand that you let us go now – and return our watches!'

The woman smiled. 'Oh, I can't do that, dear. Professor Maple will be along to explain everything in a minute – he's the Head Scientist here. In the meantime, you drink up this nice hot milk.' She looked hopefully at the games stacked up on the shelves. 'Or perhaps you could play a game? We'd love to see that …'

When the woman had gone, Cat sat in a stony mood with her arms folded. 'I'm not going to eat, drink, play or do anything while they're looking at us,' she said grumpily.

'Couldn't we just have one piece of cake?' asked Tiger. 'I'm starving!'

'Don't you dare!' Cat said, glowering.

The minutes ticked by. After a while, the door slid open again. A tall, thin scientist entered the room and smiled. He had a grey-white beard and wispy, straggling hair. Behind his wire-rimmed spectacles, his pale blue eyes were friendly.

'I am Professor Maple and I'm very pleased to meet you,' he said, holding out his hand in greeting.

Both Cat and Tiger turned away. 'Ah, I'm sorry you're so upset with us.' The professor moved the toy

rabbit and sat down in the chair. 'I'm afraid we haven't handled things very well …'

'Not *handled things very well!*' Cat was furious. 'You have trapped us, taken our watches, shut us in a glass box, and you're *observing* us without any reason!'

Professor Maple clasped his hands together. 'Surely you understand by now that there *is* a very good reason. You are the first children we have seen here in a very long time. You are very precious.'

'So we were right!' said Tiger. 'There are no other children here at all?'

'That's correct,' answered the professor. 'No children have been born here for almost five centuries. Imagine a world without the joy of children! People have become very sad and serious.'

'Wait.' Tiger was frowning. 'How have you not died out?'

The professor opened his mouth to respond but Cat interrupted. 'I still don't understand why you've had to lock us up.'

'It's for your own safety,' answered the professor. 'Once they get over their initial shock, everyone will be fascinated by you. I fear they might even fight over you.'

The professor poured himself a cup of hot milk. 'And, of course, we need to learn all about you. For instance, we'd like to know where you came from …'

At this, he shot Cat a penetrating look. Quickly, she averted her gaze.

'So you see,' Professor Maple continued amicably, 'it's best that you stay here for now and make yourselves comfortable. Anyone for cake?'

Tiger shrugged and nodded and the professor cut him a generous slice.

'I do hope you understand now,' he said, looking at Cat.

'I understand,' Cat replied. 'But I don't like it, and I don't want to be observed like a rat in a science lab.' She paused. She had been wondering how far to trust the professor and decided to take a risk. 'Professor Maple, we don't have time for all this. We're looking for someone. Can you tell me if you've ever heard of the Weaver?'

The professor looked startled, then quickly regained his composure. 'No, I haven't,' he said. 'I'm sorry.'

'Can we have our watches back?' Tiger asked.

'I'm afraid not. We don't want you to have anything that might excite you too much,' said the professor. 'However, I appreciate that you do not wish to be observed at all times. I will arrange to have the scientists observe you for only three hours a day.' With that, he stood up and left the room.

Cat and Tiger looked at each other glumly.

'Without our watches, there's nothing we can do,' said Tiger.

'Except hope that Max and Ant can rescue us,' said Cat.

Chapter 5 – Force 7 search

The security guard entered the institute, walked to the reception desk and threw his bag down on the floor. Inside the bag, micro-sized Max and Ant were crammed in against his lunchbox, shaken but unhurt. Quickly, the boys crawled out of the bag and hid behind a pot plant.

They were next to the reception desk in a vast entrance hall. Gleaming, white tiles covered the floor and the silver-painted walls shone brightly. A crowd of scientists clustered near the reception desk, staring at a large flat-screen television. By the doors, police officers patrolled up and down, their metal boots clattering loudly on the hard tiles. Over in one corner, there was a long line of elderly people queuing down a long corridor.

'Sshhhh!' Suddenly the scientists hushed each other and pointed to the television screen. Max and Ant looked up.

Across the bottom of the screen read:

Newsflash: Children spotted in Mercia.

The newsreader was talking excitedly. 'It has been confirmed that the boy and girl discovered in the museum earlier today are indeed living human children. They are currently under observation in the Institute of Regeneration.'

The screen flashed to a shot of Cat and Tiger in their room. Cat looked dejected, sitting with her head in her hands. Tiger was munching a piece of cake.

'At least we know they're OK,' Max whispered to Ant. 'And they're still in this building somewhere.'

'They're not wearing their watches!' Ant hissed.

The television was now showing an elderly couple being interviewed outside the Museum of Children.

The lady was talking. 'I still can't believe they're real. To think we were standing right next to them!' She brushed a tear from her eye. 'It's incredible!'

The newsreader was back on screen. 'Earlier, we spoke to Dr Bernwood, Deputy Head Scientist at the Institute of Regeneration.' The screen switched to a recorded interview with Dr Bernwood, a stocky man with a shock of floppy, blond hair.

'This is the most amazing thing to happen in my lifetimes,' Dr Bernwood said. 'The children are well-fed with no sign of disease. As yet, we do not know where they came from. It is possible that

someone has been caring for them in secret. We have
the children under observation and a round-the-clock
guard. We will be interviewing them in due course.'

Max recognised Dr Bernwood amongst the crowd
of scientists near the reception desk, looking smug
and self-important. He was a short man with a lab
coat that almost touched the ground.

At that moment, there was a kerfuffle at the edge of the crowd. The scientists turned away from the screen as a tall, thin man with a grey-white beard swept through the entrance hall. He had an air of authority and the crowd parted to let him through.

'How has this happened?' he shouted angrily, indicating towards the television screen. 'I gave orders for a complete news blackout. Do you understand how this information will affect people? The Institute could be overrun! It is our duty to keep these children safe. *Nobody* from this Institute should be talking to the press. *Nobody!*'

Dr Bernwood shot him a resentful look. 'Yes, Professor,' he said darkly. 'Message understood.'

Then, along with everyone else in the entrance hall, Dr Bernwood turned back to the television screen.

The newsreader was almost shouting. 'We have another urgent bulletin! Two more children were sighted today on Heston High Street. They were being brought into the Institute on a Goldflight bus when, according to the driver, they simply vanished into thin air!'

This seemed to be news to most of the scientists in reception. The hall suddenly resonated with gasps and a loud babble of voices, as everyone chattered in excitement.

'Silence!' cried the professor, and immediately the hubbub died down. 'We must remain calm. If the reports about two more children are true, Force 7 will find them. Police officers are searching the Institute, its grounds and nearby streets as we speak.'

Max noticed that many more police officers had suddenly appeared in the entrance hall. 'Thank goodness we're micro-size,' he whispered.

The professor was still talking. 'We will continue with the regeneration session this morning for those people already waiting.' He indicated towards the queue of elderly people. 'Following that, the Regeneration Lab will be closed until further notice. Now please get back to your work.'

Max whispered to Ant. 'How do you think we can rescue Cat and Tiger? We need a plan, fast!'

Ant was preoccupied as he looked up at a row of small screens with tiny numbers behind the reception desk. He used the camera on his watch to zoom in on the screens and took a couple of pictures. Eventually, he looked up. 'If we can find their watches, at least Cat and Tiger will be able to shrink,' he said. 'We'd better start searching.'

The boys carefully crept across the entrance hall, dodging the shiny, metal boots of Force 7.

'Which way?' asked Ant.

'I'm not sure,' replied Max. 'That guy they called the professor seemed to be in charge. He went up that corridor, the one where the older people are queuing. Let's try that way.'

Chapter 6 – The Regeneration Lab

Max and Ant made their way along the corridor, weaving in and out of people's feet as they tried to keep up with the professor. The queue of people ended in front of a smooth, white door.

'Let's see what's in there,' said Max.

The boys waited for a while beside an elderly lady with silvery-grey hair and a heavily wrinkled face. Eventually, the door swished open to let her through, and the boys sneaked in with her.

They found themselves in a gleaming, circular laboratory. A wide, fluorescent-green tube wound all the way round the room, like a tunnel slide in a water park. A network of thin, orange wires linked the tube to a control panel in the centre of the room.

There was no sign of the professor. Instead, Dr Bernwood stood at the control panel with another scientist by his side. He was tapping his fingers on the desk impatiently. 'Next please!' he called sharply.

The elderly lady with silvery-grey hair stepped forward obediently.

'Mrs Stokes?' said Dr Bernwood's colleague, checking the name on the computer in front of her.

The lady nodded; then she put down her handbag and shuffled nervously into the centre of the lab, using her walking stick for support. Dr Bernwood pressed a button on the control panel and a large bright-red cylinder slid out of one end of the fluorescent tube. With a sharp click, the lid of the cylinder slid back to reveal a smooth, leather bed.

'Hurry, please, Dr Jay,' said Dr Bernwood irritably. 'I have an important meeting with Professor Maple in ten minutes.'

Dr Jay helped the lady lie down inside the cylinder, strapped her in carefully and closed the lid. 'She's ready.'

Quickly, Dr Bernwood flicked a switch to lock the lid of the cylinder and tapped a code into the control panel. The cylinder shot up into the tube and around the room, its silhouette moving ominously through the tube's fluorescent-green walls.

Dr Bernwood tapped the control panel again and the cylinder slowed. A high-pitched whining noise echoed round the laboratory.

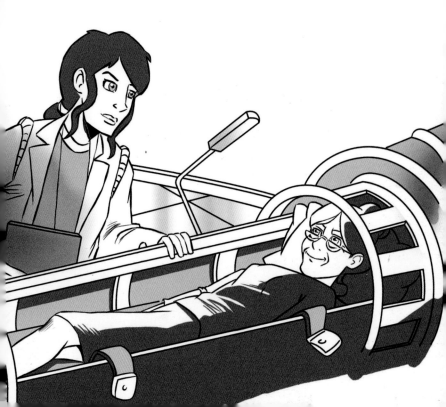

Finally, the cylinder slid smoothly out of the far end of the tube. Dr Jay hurried over as the lid opened. 'It's all done – you're ready,' she said brightly, peering inside.

What happened next was the most extraordinary thing Max and Ant had ever seen. They expected to see the elderly lady inside the cylinder. Instead, a lady about forty years younger sat up. She ran her fingers through her bouncy auburn hair, laughed in delight and stepped briskly out of the tube. Dr Jay handed her a mirror. The lady stroked the smooth skin on her face in pleasure.

'Oh, thank you,' she cried, smiling at the scientist. 'Regeneration is wonderful!'

'Your official new, fifth-life age is thirty-five,' Dr Jay told the lady, as she retrieved her handbag.

Dr Jay tapped a code into a box on the wall and a panel opened up revealing a car park outside. A Goldflight bus was waiting, packed with people in their thirties, all smiling and chattering happily. When the lady jumped on board, the bus pulled away.

Max let out a long, slow whistle. 'Can you believe it?' he asked Ant.

'I suppose it makes sense,' said Ant thoughtfully.

'There are no children in this dimension so the human race would die out as everyone grew old. The people have learned how to regenerate themselves to keep the population going.'

'Imagine how exciting it is for these people to see real children,' said Max. 'No wonder they're guarding Cat and Tiger so closely.'

'Speaking of Cat and Tiger, we're no closer to rescuing them or to finding their watches,' Ant pointed out.

'Shh!' Max hushed him.

Dr Bernwood was talking to Dr Jay. 'You'll need to regenerate the rest of the people today on your own. I need to meet Professor Maple *now!*'

'I think we'll join him,' whispered Max.

As Dr Bernwood swept out of the laboratory, the two boys caught hold of the bottom of his white coat and scrambled up into his pocket.

THE REGENERATION MACHINE

Humans in Dimension 7023 are unable to bear children. The Regeneration Machine was created to save the population.

HOW THE MACHINE WORKS:

The machine strips away layers of age. It makes hair, skin, muscles and vital organs forty years younger. A person who goes into the machine aged seventy-five will emerge from it aged thirty-five.

Limitations: The machine won't work on anyone younger than sixty-five – so it can't be used to 'make' children.

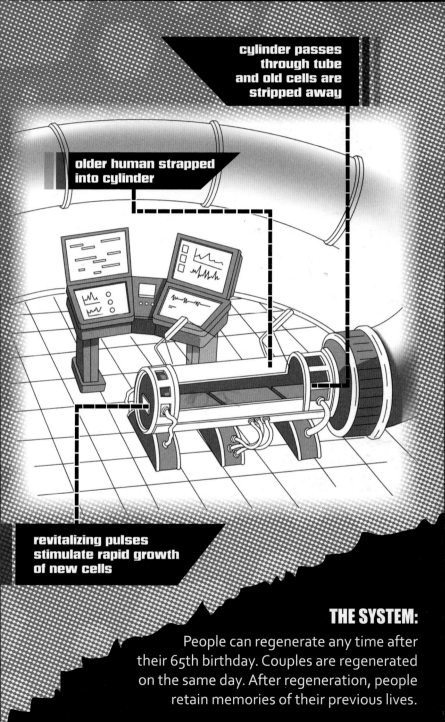

Chapter 7 – To experiment ... or not

Dr Bernwood hurried down the long, white corridor. Several Force 7 officers passed by, their boots echoing sharply on the hard tiles. Dr Bernwood turned a corner and came to Professor Maple's office. He rapped on the door and then, without waiting for an answer, marched into the room.

The boys peered out of Dr Bernwood's pocket and stared round Professor Maple's office. Unlike the rest of the institute, which was furnished in brash, grey metal, Professor Maple's office had a solid oak desk and cosy chairs. The walls were lined with shelves filled with heavy, leather books. A fire burned in the grate, and next to a small table, in front of the fire, sat Professor Maple.

'Ah, Dr Bernwood, do take a seat,' said the professor, gesturing towards a chair opposite his own. Dr Bernwood sat down, his lab coat almost reaching the floor as he did so. Max and Ant seized the opportunity, jumped out of his pocket and hid behind the chair-leg.

'Look!' Ant whispered, pointing to a glass safety box screwed to Professor Maple's desk. The boys could just glimpse the straps of Cat's and Tiger's watches inside the box.

Dr Bernwood got straight down to business. 'Professor Maple, this is a golden opportunity!' he cried, waving his hands around animatedly. 'We should be working with these children every waking moment. We need to find out where they grew up and who has looked after them. Perhaps they have been regenerated! It's so exciting!'

Professor Maple slowly shook his head. 'Dr Bernwood, as I have said before, we can't treat these children like experiments. We must treat them with kindness, give them time …'

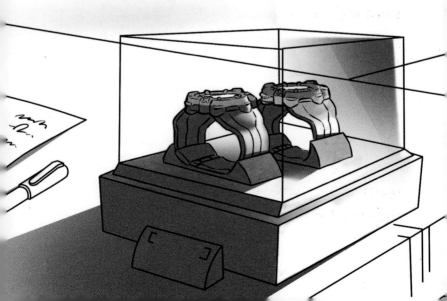

'No! We must find out everything we can and quickly!' Dr Bernwood interrupted, leaning forward earnestly. 'As you know, our abilities to regenerate are limited. We can turn the clock back forty years for people who have reached their seventy-fifth birthday – but that is all. We have not found a way to make people any younger, and we certainly can't turn adults into children.' His voice became pleading. 'Imagine how our world would be transformed if we had children in our lives again!'

Wearily, Professor Maple shook his head. 'I'm sorry. It simply cannot be,' he said softly. 'You and I have talked of this before. We can regenerate; that is enough. We do not need any more experimentation.'

Dr Bernwood banged his fist on the table in frustration. 'You are wrong, Professor! We must develop our research.' His eyes flashed manically. 'We could even try to regenerate one of the children … perhaps turn it into a baby!'

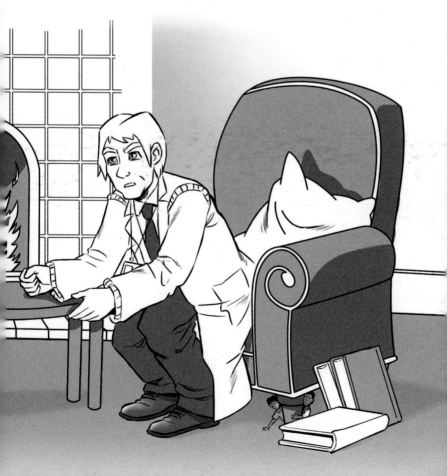

'Absolutely not!' Professor Maple roared, his mild blue eyes now blazing. 'I do not want to hear such talk again.'

Angrily, Dr Bernwood pushed back his chair and stormed out of the room. Professor Maple sighed heavily, then he picked up some papers and left his office.

'Now's our chance,' said Ant, scrolling through the photos on his watch. 'Max, while we were in reception, I saw codes to open all the rooms in the building. Look, here's the number for the observation room.' Ant showed Max the image.

'Ant, you're a genius!' cried Max.

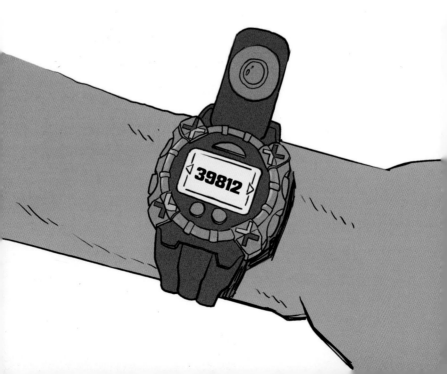

'Can you memorize the number?' asked Ant. 'You can rescue Cat and Tiger while I focus on their watches. I'll have to try to work out how to get into the box.'

Max stared at the number for the observation room and committed it to memory. 'OK, I've got it,' he said.

'Look at the map on the wall over there,' said Ant. 'It shows the whole building. Can you see the observation room on it?'

Max examined the map. 'Yes – I'll find the way,' he said, heading for the door.

'Let's meet in the Regeneration Lab,' Ant called after him.

Taking a deep breath, Max set out on his long journey across the building, running the code through his mind over and over again.

Chapter 8 – Rescue

Max stood outside the door to the observation room, panting hard. It had seemed to take forever to work his way through the maze of white corridors, dodging patrolling Force 7 officers, but he had got there in the end. He pushed the button on his watch and grew back to normal size so that he'd be able to reach the keypad.

For a moment, Max's mind went blank and he panicked. He'd forgotten the code! He took a few deep breaths to calm himself then visualized the numbers on Ant's watch. Slowly, the numbers swam into focus in his mind, and he punched the code into the keypad: *3 9 8 1 2 ...*

The door slid open. Cat and Tiger were slumped in two armchairs, idly flicking through books.

When he saw his friend, Tiger tossed his book to one side and jumped up excitedly. 'What took you so long?'

'Max, they've taken our watches!' Cat said urgently.

'I know. We can talk later,' replied Max quickly.

'We've got to get out of here now. Follow me and keep quiet. The building is crawling with police officers.'

Cautiously, Max peered up and down the corridor. It was clear. He crept out and beckoned to Cat and Tiger to follow him.

All of a sudden, a siren blared through the building. *Whoop! Whoop!* Terrified, Max froze. He could hear hundreds of pairs of boots clattering down the corridor towards the observation room. Something must have gone wrong. He shook himself. *Come on,* Max thought. *We just need to find Ant and then we can get out of here.*

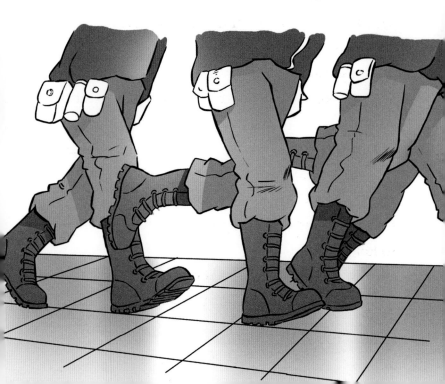

'Run!' Max shouted, leading the way and trying to remember the layout of the building. Cat and Tiger raced after him.

Two Force 7 officers pounded into the corridor ahead. Max took a sharp right into a small, narrow passage and the others followed just in the nick of time.

'That was close,' said Tiger, panting. 'I don't think they saw us.'

The narrow passage twisted and turned through the heart of the building. The children raced on like mice in a maze. Every so often, they looked through openings into the main corridors where lights were blazing and police officers and scientists were hurrying to and fro.

Close by, Ant was haring towards the Regeneration Lab, too, his heart pounding. He glanced over his shoulder to see two Force 7 police officers closing in fast. He felt terrified and guilty that he'd bungled the plan. He had been sure he'd worked out the code for the safety box but, as soon as he'd entered the number, the alarm had sounded. He just hoped his friends were all right as he sprinted on down the corridor.

Then Ant rounded a corner and collided with

someone. The air was knocked from his lungs and he tripped and fell to the ground, dazed. For a horrible, confused moment, Ant thought he'd run into one of the Force 7 officers, but then he felt friendly hands pulling him quickly to his feet.

'Ant!' Cat shouted. 'Run!'

The friends heard a shout from behind. 'Stop there!'

Reunited, the four friends sped down the last part of the corridor. Their luck didn't hold. As they approached the entrance to the Regeneration Lab, three more Force 7 police officers appeared in the doorway, blocking the route.

'Shrink now!' Max cried.

Cat held Ant's arm as he pressed the button on his watch, shrinking both of them simultaneously. Max reached for Tiger but, as Max pressed his watch, Tiger tripped and fell out of his grasp. Max shrank but Tiger remained normal size.

Helplessly, Max watched his friend struggle to his feet. Then, as one of the Force 7 police officers lunged forwards, Tiger darted to one side. Before the officer realized what had happened, Tiger sprinted into the Regeneration Lab.

The corridor was now full of Force 7 police officers and scientists, all shouting at each other in confusion.

Then someone pointed to the Regeneration Lab.

'At least one of them went that way. Search the room!'

Horrified, the three micro-friends flattened themselves against the wall as four police officers marched past them and into the laboratory. They waited with a sinking feeling, expecting a Force 7 police officer to come out with Tiger in his grasp. However, after a while, all four officers emerged looking puzzled and confused.

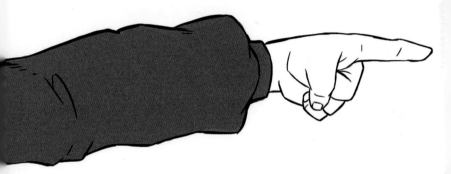

'There's no one in there,' said one of the officers. 'It's unbelievable! The children have just disappeared. We'll have to report this to Professor Maple.'

The police officers marched off down the corridor. When they were sure all the Force 7 patrols had gone, Max, Cat and Ant entered the Regeneration Lab. Astonished, they stared all around. The police officers were right: Tiger had disappeared.

Chapter 9 – A close encounter

'Did Tiger shrink?' asked Cat, turning to Ant. 'Did you give him his watch somehow?'

'I didn't get the watches.' Ant looked at Max despondently. 'I'm sorry – I thought I'd worked out the code for the box but I must have made a mistake. It set the alarm off.'

'Then where did Tiger go?' Cat was perplexed.

Max pointed to the closed red cylinder which was parked at the bottom of the fluorescent tube. 'If I know Tiger, he'll be hiding … most likely in there. Of course, he doesn't know what it is …'

Cat was about to ask Max to explain when Dr Bernwood stepped out from the shadows in the corner of the room. He looked around surreptitiously, then he dashed to the control panel and flicked a switch to lock the lid of the cylinder.

'I've got you, boy!' he cried gleefully. 'Now everybody's out of the way, I can experiment.' He switched on the Regeneration Machine and touched the control panel, his eyes glittering with excitement.

Max watched in horror as the Regeneration Machine began to hum and fizz.

'Ready!' cried Dr Bernwood triumphantly. 'Let's see what happens!' His hand hovered over the *on* switch for the red cylinder – then, as he was about to bring his hand down, the door to the Regeneration Lab shot open.

Professor Maple strode into the room. 'Ah, Dr Bernwood! What are you doing here? I thought I'd given orders for the Regeneration Lab to be shut down for the rest of today.'

For a moment, Dr Bernwood was lost for words. Then he recovered himself. 'I … I'm assisting in the search for the missing children, Professor Maple. They were last seen near this room, I believe.'

'Indeed they were,' answered the Professor, 'but you can leave the searching to Force 7. I'm sure the children will be found before long.' His eyes flickered over the control panel, taking everything in. 'In the meantime, Dr Bernwood, I suggest you retire to your apartment and take a rest.'

Resentfully, Dr Bernwood stalked out of the room.

Professor Maple waited until his colleague was gone, then went to the door and pressed a silver button to lock it. He walked over to the control panel and flicked the switch to open the red cylinder.

'All right, you can come out now,' he said. The micro-friends gasped as Tiger sat up, looking petrified. Then, to their astonishment, Professor Maple turned and spoke to the seemingly empty room. 'You three might as well come out now, too. I need to talk to you all together.'

Max, Cat and Ant looked at each other in alarm.

'What shall we do?' whispered Ant.

'We don't have much choice,' Max muttered. 'We can't leave this dimension without our watches and we'll need some help to get them back.'

'Besides, he saved Tiger from Dr Bernwood, didn't he?' added Cat. 'I say we trust him.'

'OK,' said Max. 'Grow!'

Professor Maple looked startled when the three friends grew in front of him. 'Goodness, there are so many things I don't know about you,' he said. Then he gazed at the friends for a long time. Cat thought she saw tears in his thoughtful, blue eyes.

'Forgive me,' the Professor said eventually. 'Before today, I hadn't seen human children for many years. It is simply wonderful to see all four of you together.' He smiled at Max and Ant. 'It's a pleasure to meet you.'

Max stepped forward. 'It's good to meet you, too, Professor. However, my friends and I need to be on our way. Could you please return Cat and Ant's watches?'

Professor Maple nodded, thoughtfully. 'I will, but first I think it is time for me to introduce myself properly.'

To the children's surprise, the professor took off his glasses and unbuttoned his white lab coat. Then he shook it off to reveal a grey, shimmering tunic woven from fine wool.

'My name is Floros,' he said with a flourish. 'I am a rip-traveller.'

Chapter 10 – The rip-traveller

'What?' asked Tiger, looking at Floros in wonder.

Ant looked thoughtful. 'Does that mean you know all about the rips and the different dimensions?'

'I do,' answered Floros. 'As a rip-traveller I used to move freely between the dimensions, though I have been in **7023** for many long years.'

'Have you ever heard of the Weaver?' Max asked. 'We came here to find him.'

Floros turned to Cat. 'I must apologise for not answering your question honestly earlier,' he said. 'At that point, I was still not sure whether to trust you. The truth is, I have heard of the Weaver. It's possible he travelled this way many centuries ago.'

'Centuries?' repeated Tiger, disappointed.

'Do you know where he is now?' asked Cat hopefully.

'Ah, no … I haven't spoken to anyone from another dimension for so long. After I arrived in Dimension **7023**, I stayed on because I felt sorry for the people here. They had become unable to bear children. They were in danger of dying out! I decided to find a way to help.'

Ant clicked his fingers and pointed at Floros. 'You built the Regeneration Machine!' he surmised.

'Yes. After many years of experimentation, I managed to enable the people to regenerate. Life isn't perfect here but at least the people go on living.'

At this point, Floros sighed deeply. 'After building the machine, I intended to leave this dimension, but I was dismayed to find I could no longer rip-travel. My rip-passport was jammed. I guessed that was because dark things were happening in other worlds. Since then, I have lived for all these years with no news of other dimensions – except for one passing visitor. That is, until you came along ...' Floros looked at the children shrewdly. 'I assume you arrived here through a rip?'

Max nodded. Then he told Floros about their rip-jumping adventures and about how their rip had grown bigger and bigger. He described how the Krush had arrived in their dimension.

As Max spoke, Floros kept shaking his head. 'This is grim news indeed,' he said, when Max mentioned the Krush. 'I have never come across these Krush but they sound terrible. I fear they will be far more dangerous if they enter your dimension a second time. You must get home.'

Max went on to explain how Perlest had come through Tiger's wardrobe.

At the mention of Perlest, Floros jumped. 'Perlest!' he cried. 'She was my one visitor over these many lonely years – the last person I saw from another dimension! She, too, came looking for the Weaver.' Floros smiled. 'I'm glad you mentioned her name. She left something for me to keep safely; it might help you now. Wait here; you'd better lock the door after me.' He put on his white coat and left the chamber.

To the friends, it seemed ages before the rip-traveller returned. Once again, they could hear Force 7 stamping in the corridors. Finally, there was a tap on the door. Max opened it carefully. Floros walked in with the watches and what looked like a small bottle which he handed to Cat. 'This is what Perlest gave me for safe-keeping. You must take it to her now.'

Floros also gave Cat and Tiger their watches. Then, looking almost sheepish, he asked, 'Do you mind if I follow you through the rip? I won't come to your dimension. I'll go elsewhere – where I might be needed in these dark times.'

'What about the people in this dimension?' asked Ant. 'How will they cope with Dr Bernwood?'

'Oh, I've just promoted Dr Jay. She'll be the next Head Scientist,' Floros replied. 'I'm sure she'll keep Bernwood under control. I have done all I can here.'

The children held up their watches and turned the dials. Blue energy lines surged from each screen and joined together. The rip began to fizz and crackle and the children stepped through. The rip-traveller followed close behind, disappearing off on an adventure of his own.

Epilogue

The friends slid out of the rip into Tiger's bedroom where Perlest was waiting for them.

'Where is the Weaver?' Perlest demanded harshly, when she realized the children had come home alone.

'We didn't find him in Dimension **7023**,' said Max. Perlest's face darkened.

Cat spoke quickly. 'But we did find a rip-traveller. He said he knew you. He gave us this to give back to you …' She handed the bottle to Perlest.

Perlest's face brightened as she cradled it in her hands. 'Do you know what this is?' she asked the friends. She pulled the cork out of the vial and a sweet aroma filled the room. Thin strands of smoke drifted out of the bottle and floated into the air above. 'It's a thought vial,' said Perlest. 'Watch.'

Gradually, the strands of smoke formed into a picture and, after a few moments, the picture became a moving image of an ocean. There was nothing else but the aqua-blue water of the ocean. Sounds of gently lapping waves filled Tiger's bedroom.

Perlest's eyes narrowed then softened. 'Ah … it's coming back to me now. This is not the first time I've had to look for the Weaver …'

'What do you mean?' Cat asked. 'Why didn't you tell us this before?'

'Because these thoughts have been lost to me for many years,' Perlest told her.

'Lost? How?' asked Ant.

'Long ago, during the First Dimension War, I suffered greatly, as did many others,' replied Perlest. 'I was worried that my thoughts would be stolen from me. So I stored some of them about the Weaver and left them with others for safe keeping.'

'So are these thoughts a clue to where the Weaver might be?' asked Tiger.

'They are,' Perlest confirmed. 'This vial shows Dimension **4455** – the Dimension of Memories. I believe you'll find another thought vial there.'

'Then that's where we need to go next,' said Max, with a new-found determination. He set the dial on his watch, tapped in the numbers **4455** and took a deep breath, preparing himself for the next rip-jump.

NEXT ... The Sea of Memories